AF601909

EJ and the Season That Changed Everything

A story about patience, perseverance, and purpose

Melissa Richey-Bridges & Edwin Bridges, Jr.

ISBN 979-8-9927360-6-9

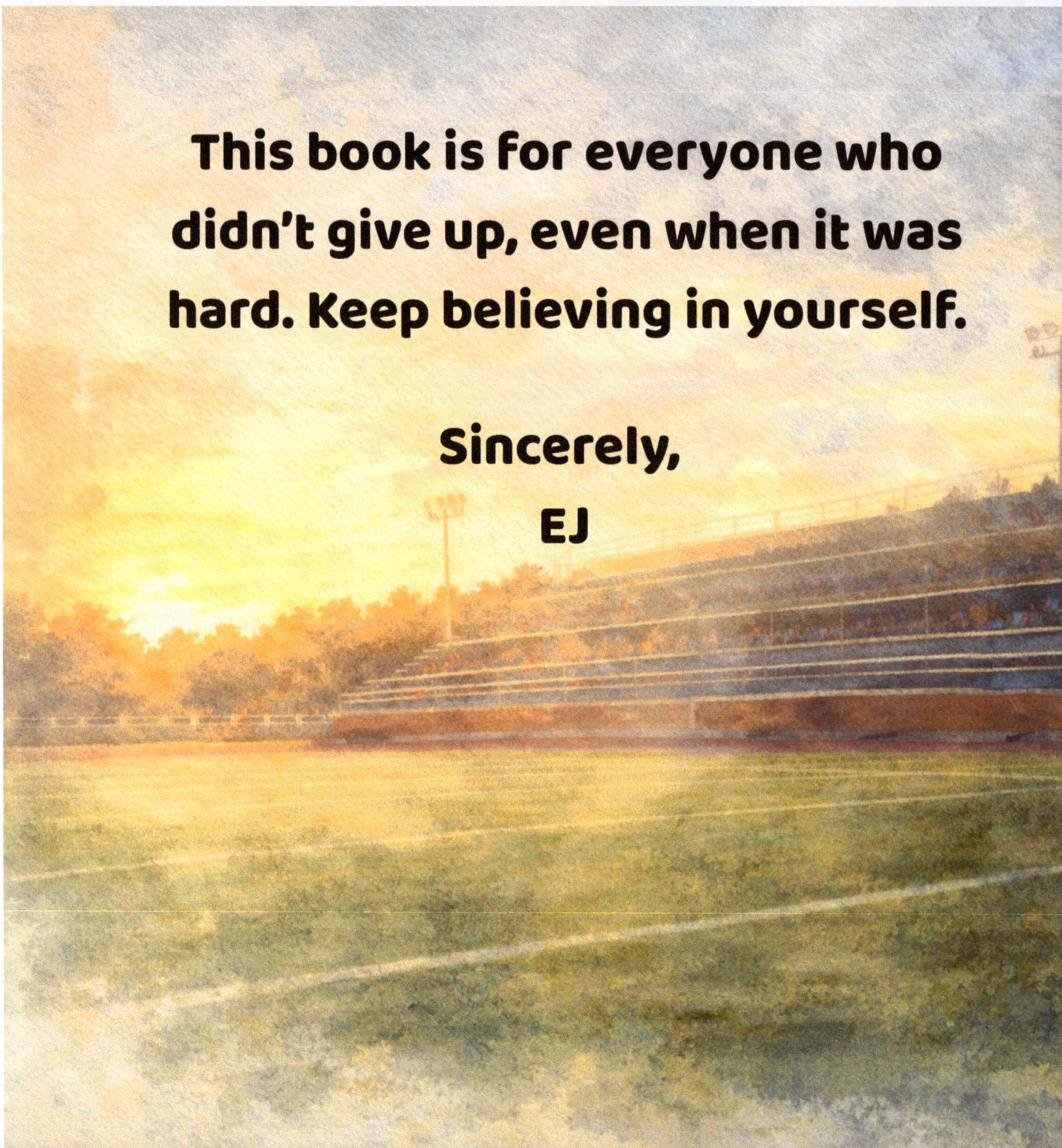

This book is for everyone who didn't give up, even when it was hard. Keep believing in yourself.

Sincerely,

EJ

Meet
EJ
35

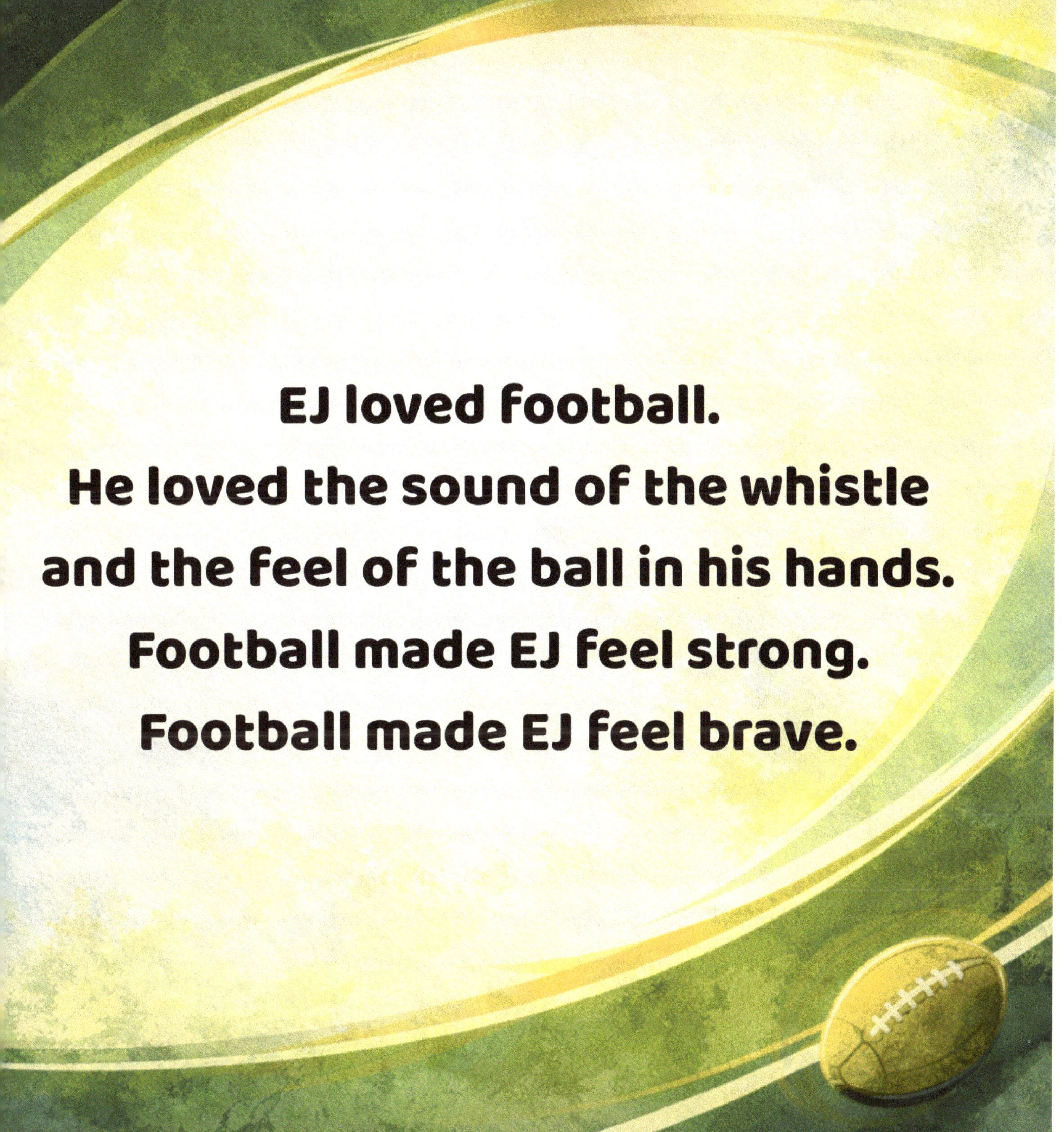

EJ loved football.
He loved the sound of the whistle
and the feel of the ball in his hands.
Football made EJ feel strong.
Football made EJ feel brave.

A Tough Season

EJ worked hard at practice.
He listened.
He showed up every day.
But one year, EJ didn't get much time in the game.
He watched from the sidelines.
He waited.
Sometimes EJ felt sad.
Sometimes he felt invisible.

35
Big Feelings,
Quiet Strength

EJ lived with his dad.

He missed his mom.

His dad reminded him,

"Your time will come. Keep your heart right."

They prayed together.

They believed together.

Still Showing Up

Even when EJ wasn't playing much, he kept trying.

He ran every drill.

He cheered for his teammates.

He stayed ready.

EJ learned that effort always matters, even when no one is watching.

But One Day, It All Changed

One day, the coach called EJ's name.

"EJ...you're in."

EJ's heart started beating fast.
His cleats touched the field.
This was his moment.

Running With Purpose

EJ lined up as the running back.

The ball was snapped.

Yard after yard, snap after snap,

EJ kept running.

Touchdown after touchdown,

EJ kept believing.

EJ wasn't just running with his legs, he was running with his heart.

A Friday Night to Remember

One Friday night, EJ ran like never before.
He rushed for 229 yards.
He scored two touchdowns.
The crowd cheered.
His team celebrated.
His mom was there, she was so proud.
EJ helped lead his team to a big victory.

More Than a Win

After the game, EJ was named Most Valuable Player.

He helped lead his team to the playoffs.

Unfortunately, they didn't win, but they built something special.

They built trust.

They built character.

They built a bond that would last forever.

The Highest Honor

At the end of the season, EJ was honored for his hard work.

For his effort.

For his patience.

For never giving up.

EJ was named Offensive Player of the Year!

EJ learned that waiting seasons don't weaken you, they prepare you.

The Real Victory

EJ smiled.

Not because of trophies.

Not because of applause.

But because he stayed ready

when the wait was hard.

Sometimes the biggest victories come

after the longest waits.

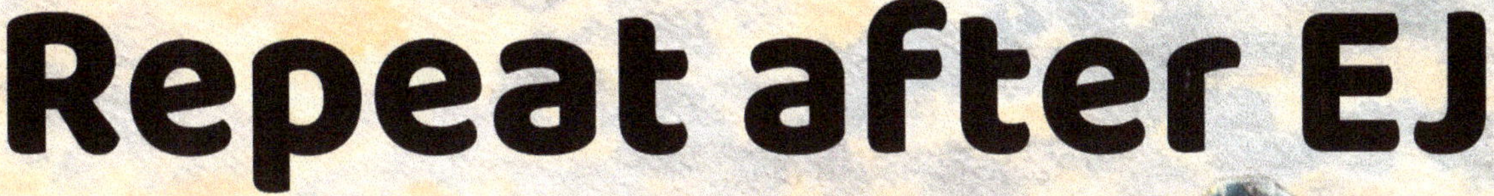

Repeat after EJ

I am strong.

I am patient.

I don't give up.

God sees me.

My time will come.

A Note from EJ

My senior season of football taught me lessons I will carry for the rest of my life. I learned that you will not always get the results you want, and when you do, they will not come on your timing, but on God's timing. I learned that respect is earned through effort, consistency, and performance. I also learned that it is never too late to try something new. And most of all, I learned that sometimes you don't realize you're making some of your best memories until the season is over.

About the Co-Author

EJ Bridges is a student-athlete whose journey taught him the importance of patience, perseverance, and purpose. Through football, EJ learned that success doesn't always come right away, but hard work and determination are always worth it. This book is inspired by EJ's real-life experiences and is written to encourage kids to stay focused, trust their growth, and never give up on their goals.

www.ingramcontent.com/pod-product-compliance
Ingram Content Group UK Ltd.
Pitfield, Milton Keynes, MK11 3LW, UK
UKHW052224270726
14059UKWH00003B/105

9 798992 736069